D0014702

CONTENTS

Pictorial Credits
Black and white: Al Barry: 35 (4); George D. Cowderry: 25 (5); Robert P. Hammond: 16 (1); Lilo Hess: 48; Herman Hiller: 35 (8); Harry V. Lacey: 5, 16 (4, 5, 6, 7, 9), 24 (6, 7, 8); 29, 34, 35 (1, 2, 3, 5, 9), 45, 46, 49, 53, 54, 55, 73 (3, 4, 6, 7, 8), 77, 92; Louise van der Meid: 16 (7, 8, 10), 24 (4), 51 (4), 52, 60; George P. Nicholas: 35 (6), George Pickow: 35 (7), 51 (3); G.J.M. Timmerman: 51 (4), Walter Pieschel: 35 (10).

Color: Harry V. Lacey: Cover, front endpapers, 2, 3, 6, 7, 14, 15, 18, 22, 26, 27, 30, 31, 66, 67, 70, 71, 75, 78, 79; Louise van der Meid: 10, 74; Horst Mueller: 82, 83, 86, 87, 90, 91.

© 1979 by T.F.H. Publications, Inc., Ltd.

ISBN 0-87666-983-6 • KW-004

Distributed in the U.S. by T.F.H. Publications, Inc., 211 West Sylvania Avenue, P.O. Box 427, Neptune, N.J. 07753; in England by T.F.H. (Gt. Britain) Ltd., 13 Nutley Lane, Reigate, Surrey; in Canada to the book store and library trade by Beaverbooks, 953 Dillingham Road, Pickering, Ontario L1W 1Z7; in Canada to the pet trade by Rolf C. Hagen Ltd., 3225 Sartelon Street, Montreal 382, Quebec; in Southeast Asia by Y.W. Ong, 9 Lorong 36 Geylang, Singapore 14; in Australia and the South Pacific by Pet Imports Pty. Ltd., P.O. Box 149, Brookvale 2100, N.S.W., Australia; in South Africa by Valiant Publishers (Pty.) Ltd., P.O. Box 78236, Sandton City, 2146, South Africa; Published by T.F.H. Publications, Inc., Ltd., The British Crown Colony of Hong Kong.

CANARIES

edited by **PAUL PARADISE**

A pair of variegated Gloster Fancy canaries.

Introduction

A pair of Crested Canaries. This bird is sometimes still known as the Crested Norwich, from which breed they sprang over a century ago. This pair consists of a Crested individual and a Plainhead.

HISTORY

In 1478 the Spaniards conquered the Canary Islands, off the coast of Africa. What enchanted the sailors the most on these islands were the beautiful singing birds, and within a few years canaries became a great favorite among the rich in Europe. The earliest reference to the canary is in Gesner's *Historia Animalium* in 1555.

Although there are many different colors and sizes of canary today, the one the Spaniards exported stood about four inches in length and was a greenish yellow color. The Spaniards maintained a monopoly on the sale of canaries for over a hundred years by selling only male birds. In the 16th century, however, a Spanish ship laden with a cargo of canaries was wrecked and many of the birds which escaped managed to reach the island of Elba. The Italians soon capitalized on this 'historical accident,' and soon these birds were being shipped all over Europe, where French, Dutch and German birdkeepers learned the secrets of breeding them.

Most varieties of canaries have been classified according to their shape and have been named after the geographical area in which they were developed; for example, the Yorkshire, the Norwich and the Border (named after the Border Counties of England and Scotland). Other varieties are named for the plumage pattern, song and color; for example, the Roller Canary, named for its song, and the Lizard, named for its distinctive color pattern.

By the eighteenth century, canaries had become numerous enough for all levels of society to own. Different countries became exclusive in the qualities they were breeding for. The Germans bred for better song quality; the English were more interested in fancy color varieties; and the French developed over 27 individual varieties of canary distinguished by the color of their plumage.

BUYING A CANARY

As a general rule the best and most reliable source for birds is the pet shop owner. Most owners prefer a male since only the males will sing. The price the dealer charges will be reasonable since it is based on going competitive prices. Canaries come in a variety of colors, from deep orange to light red, yellow, white and blue-and-white. The more red in a canary, the more valuable it is. The Red Factor canaries are the most expensive.

Always listen to the birds before purchasing, because canaries differ quite a bit as to song. The Roller Canaries have a song that sounds like a trill or roll. The Chopper Canaries have a song that is very romantic in tune. All male singing canaries are kept separated from each other so they may not sing in answer to other birds' calls.

If buying a bird from other than a pet shop, the best source would be private breeders who advertise their birds in the cage bird magazines. *American Cage-Bird Magazine,* which is based at 3449 North Western Avenue, Chicago, Illinois, and *Cage and Aviary Birds,* Surrey House 1

Throwley Way, Sutton, Surrey, England, both contain advertisements and tips on canaries.

Inspect the bird before you buy it. The bird should have an alert disposition. If it sits on its perch with its wings puffed up, it may be sick. This puffed-up condition is so that the bird will retain its body heat. The eyes and nose should not be runny. Look at the floor of the cage and be sure that the droppings are well formed and black and white. Green-white droppings are indicative of sickness, usually diarrhea.

THE BIRD IN THE HOME

When you arrive home with the bird you've selected, you should have the cage already set up, with the following items ready:

1. Canary seed (the everyday food for the bird).
2. Egg biscuit ('cake' for your bird).
3. White bird grit with charcoal (canaries need the grit to digest their food).
4. Cuttlebone (to supply the calcium requirements for fine development).
5. A bird bath (to keep your canary clean).
6. Paper (for the bottom of the cage).
7. Treat cup (for song food and biscuit).
8. Cage cover (to protect your bird from drafts and disturbances).

A roomy cage will be easier to clean. It should be hung on a stand or wall bracket, not placed on the floor. The cage should be free from drafts and gas fumes. When the bird arrives home the drinker should be filled with water that is not too hot nor too cold. One of the small treat cups should be filled with egg biscuit and squeezed through the bars of the cage. Put the special cage carpet on the floor of the cage. Sprinkle some white bird grit and charcoal over it.

When the cage is ready, open the door and bring the carrying box with the canary next to it. Open the door of the

Red Factor Canary. A frosted opal bronze cock. The melanin pigments are very much diluted in this mutation.

Opposite:
Clear buff Norwich Canary cock. This bird is known as the 'John Bull' of the Fancy; as the name implies, it is thickset and stocky, with a broad back.

carton so that the bird can jump from the dark box into its new home. If the bird is afraid to jump out, then place your hand in gently and grasp the canary fully about his body and place him inside. To hold or grasp a bird the fingers should wrap around the bird's body over the wings; the thumb and forefinger should be around the sides of the head, so it will not turn and bite. Canaries rarely bite, and even if they do they never break the skin.

THE AVIARY

For breeders or owners of many birds the aviary is a useful structure. It consists of two sections: the birdhouse and the flight. The birdhouse is a covered structure usually made of wood, while the flight is an exercise area usually made of wire. The floors are usually made of cement. Heating and lighting can be added.

The mesh for the aviary is usually about 3/8th of an inch. The cost of mesh is based on the weight of the wire and the size of the mesh. If mesh much larger than the size given is used, mice will be able to sneak into the aviary.

CLEANING AND FEEDING

Cleanliness is all important. Most diseases can be related to not keeping a regular cleaning schedule. Keep your bird clean and well fed and you have a 100% chance of never having troubles.

With a layer of white bird grit on the bottom of the cage (about 1/8" thick), it will only be necessary to clean the cage every two or three days. The gravel acts as an absorbent and the wastes will not have any odor nor will they contaminate the cage. If you have carefully placed the wooden perches in the cage so that the bird's droppings do not fall into its food or water, then you will save yourself a lot of work and money. Give the bird fresh, clean water every day and rinse the cup out before each watering. Replace the seed in the seed cup every day, throwing away the old seed and replacing it with fresh seed. The treat cup should be filled one day with biscuit and the next day with song food.

Normally a canary will eat about a teaspoonful of seed every day, so put in a teaspoon and a half so you are sure he has enough food. Be sure your seed is fresh. It should be shiny, clean and dry. Smelly food or damp food should be thrown out and fresh seed purchased. You can ensure the freshness of your seed if you keep it in a glass jar rather than a bag or paper box.

Feed your canary the food it has been accustomed to eating. Changing the seed may throw your bird "off its feed."

For variety, add a bit of sweet peeled apple to the bird's diet by squeezing it through the wire bars of the cage. Dandelions (both flowers and greens), lettuce and oranges are eaten ravenously by canaries, but they should only be offered sparingly.

Watch the bird's droppings very closely when you offer these fresh foods. Very often it loosens their bowels and then trouble might start. As the droppings loosen up, stop feeding the fresh foods. Cuttlebone, the white chalk-like "bone" of a squid, should always be hanging in the cage for the bird to peck at and clean its bill upon. The lime in the bone is helpful in digestion, too, and it is a good cure for loose droppings. No need to worry about the bird eating too much cuttlebone!

If you notice that your bird eats all the seed you are offering it, then increase the amount of seed. The canary will not overeat.

Never let a canary go without water. They will not live for 24 hours without water to drink.

To aid the bird in keeping itself clean, it is advisable to get a bird bath. Bird baths can be fancy glass or plastic enclosures which allow the bird to enter, splash about to its heart's content and shake the water from its feathers, all in the protected enclosure so your floor is not splattered. A

Cinnamon Border Fancy canary. This color mutation lacks any black pigmentation, its 'cinnamon' coloring being produced by brown melanin upon the yellow lipochrome ground color.

Opposite:
The Yorkshire Canary is known as the 'Gentleman of the Fancy.' this bird is a grand canary, but is now quite different from those that were kept many years ago. In those days it was a very slim bird but is now a stout bird.

15

1

4

2

5

7

8

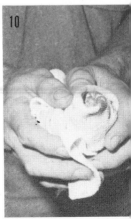

9

3

10

6

16

Opposite:
1. All-metal cages are probably the easiest of all cages to clean. 2. The best grades of seeds cost less in the long run; you are sure of getting properly cleaned and dust-free seed. 3. Roller canaries are fed more rape seed than canary seed, the idea being to keep them less stimulated and their song softer. 4. The Border Fancy was produced first in the British Isles. 5. A baby Lizard enjoying its daily ration of greenfood. 6. The Norwich cock (next to a Bullfinch hen) is known as being a fairly good singer of the chopper song and is a tame and steady bird, although lazy in some respects. 7. Cuttlebones are mostly calcium, and this is present in a readily digestible form. 8. The best time for a canary to bathe is right after you clean his cage, because this is when he prefers to bathe most. Usually a canary will bathe more readily in an oval bath set on the cage floor, but if it can be induced to enter an outside bath, one that hangs on the outside of his cage door, so much the better. 9. Often it takes some birds quite a while to get used to outside-of-cage baths; they seem afraid of them. Sometimes if you place a little green food in the shallow water, it will help matters. 10. Never force a canary into the bath. If it won't bathe, don't worry; spray non-bathing birds with an atomizer, but do this only early in the morning and when the room is warm.

---

shallow dish of water (at room temperature) placed in the bottom of the cage will serve the same purpose, though after the bath it will be necessary to change the cage bottom. In the long run it is simpler to get a special bird bath. Many varieties are available at reasonable prices.

Your bird should be allowed to bathe every morning in the summer so he will have dried out his feathers by the time he roosts at night. In the winter if his room is cold, do not allow him to bathe. If your bird won't bathe by himself, squirt a little water on him from time to time, and pretty soon he will get the idea and join the splashing party.

Canaries should be groomed, just like any other animal. Their nails need clipping, and sometimes their dead feathers must be pulled out. Leave this job to an expert. Ask your canary salesman to do the job. If no one is available, then hold the bird on its back and carefully clip the nail about 1/8″ above the fine vein that runs into the nail. Do not cut the vein or the bird might bleed to death.

17

Clear buff Norwich
Canary cock.

Canary
Varieties

Five-week-old
Yorkshire Canaries.

THE GLOSTER FANCY CANARY

This is a modern breed of canary. At the Crystal Palace Show in 1925, a Mrs. Rogerson of Cheltenham, Gloucestershire, England, showed two miniature Crest Canaries that so impressed the Show Manager, the late Mr. A. Smith, that he used his influence to encourage their development and named the birds Glosters in honor of Mrs. Rogerson.

These birds proved most successful with instant appeal to the ladies, being dainty little birds with a neat feather corona on top of their heads. Within a very short period of time they had become the second most popular canary in Britain.

The Gloster should not exceed 4½ inches in length for show purposes. They are quite inexpensive to buy, and a pair capable of breeding winners can be purchased at a modest price. They are very free breeders and make excellent birds for the beginner.

There are two types of Gloster Canary, the Corona, which carries the crest, and the Consort, with the plain head. It is essential that a Corona be paired with a Consort to retain the neat corona. It is immaterial which sex is the Corona and which is the Consort, and both types may be produced. Pairing two Consorts would produce only plainhead offspring; unfortunately, due to their make-up, 25% of the offspring of two Crested birds would die either in their shell or shortly after hatching.

The aim of the Gloster breeder is for a bird with a tendency towards the diminutive, but this does not mean that the bird should be small. It should be well built and cobby, not mean or racy in any way. The neck, back and chest should be well filled and the flights should be closely braced to the body with the tips just meeting. The bird should stand at an angle of 45 degrees and its action should be similar to that of a Border Fancy. The Gloster is not color fed and it is therefore very important that a good, sound natural color be obtained when purchased. The corona should radiate evenly around the head of the bird from the center, where no 'hole' should appear. Unlike the Crest Canary, the corona should not obscure the eyes, which should be clear and bright. Any roughness at the back of the skull running into the neck must be avoided, and the head should be bold and well rounded. A coarse beak detracts from the general appearance of the bird and therefore a short, neat beak should always be aimed for.

THE BORDER FANCY CANARY

This is the most popular canary on the show bench today. It is, in fact, the layman's picture of what a canary should look like. Originally known as the Cumberland Fancy, it was bred and developed in the Border Counties of England and Scotland. The Border is a very free breeder and can be recommended for the beginner.

Earlier this century the Border Fancy was the smallest type of show canary and was known as the 'Wee Gem,' but since the advent of the Gloster and Fife Fancy not much has been heard of this expression. For show purposes, the Border Fancy should not be more than 5½ inches long and should look 'round' from whatever angle it is viewed. Feather is most important and should be short and silky. Coarse-feathered birds will not be tolerated.

Unfortunately, due to mistakes made by breeders in the 1940's when large-sized birds were in favor, many undesirable traits have been introduced into the Border Fancy that crop up to frustrate the Border breeder of today. The lack of rounded backs, necks that are too short, heads that are pinched in, and poor feather quality are often evident in even the most carefully bred stocks.

The Border Fancy requires considerably more training than the Gloster as it is a bird of action and should move from perch to perch in the show cage with a lively, jaunty action leaving plenty of daylight between the perch and its belly. A bird that is low on the perch or one that tips over the perch when alighting would be faulted by the judge in a show, so it is essential that a bird be well trained.

THE YORKSHIRE

Known as the 'Gentleman of the Fancy,' the Yorkshire is a grand bird, but it is now quite different from those that were kept many years ago. In those days it was a very slim bird; today it is a stout bird with length and long legs.

The Yorkshire Canary was mentioned as far back as the early 1860's but the present day Yorkshire was produced by crossing the common canary with the Lancashire to give it length and size, the Norwich to give it color and quality of

Yorkshire Canary. The blue variegated white bird shows particularly
well the offending twisted feathers around the throat.

A fine study of a blue Border Canary. Border breeders are keen on a bird that is as near to blue as possible.

feather, and the Belgium to give it verve and swagger. With such a diverse heritage, breeders were uncertain as to type and markings for a long time.

The Specialist Yorkshire Canary Societies have laid down rules for the different classes at the shows and birds are classified according to the dark feathers known as the 'technical marks' which they carry. These consist of dark feathers touching the eyes, flight feathers on both wings, and either side of the tail. No other marks on the bird's body count at all. These marks apply only when the patronage of a Yorkshire Specialist Society has been given. They are most confusing to the novice and even the champions slip up at times and it is possible for a bird to carry a mass of dark feathers on its back and breast and yet be classed as a clear or ticked bird.

THE NORWICH CANARY

This grand bird is known as the 'John Bull' of the Fancy and as the name implies, it is thick and stocky with a broad

Opposite:
1-5. There are literally dozens of different designs in cages for canaries. The all-metal cages, especially when one has a lot of birds, are the best. The smaller all-wire cages can be obtained at very reasonable cost in all pet stores. Some of the latest models have hinged tops that swing open, making interior cleaning easier. Also, these cages can be folded flat for easy storage when not in use. Some have two sets of seed and water cups, which are handy; soiled ones can be sterilized while clean ones are in use. 6. Border Fancy Canary. A wing-marked yellow cock. 7. Border Fancy Canary. A nice self green. Border canaries are the most popular breed of canaries in Great Britain. A little larger in size than the chopper and roller breeds, it is a well-shaped and fairly chubby bird, with a well-rounded head and large, bold eyes. It is similar in appearance to the Norwich canary, but smaller. 8. Yellow canaries are common birds. The mottled bird is a cross between a canary and a linnet.

24

Left: a frosted golden green satinette. Right: a non-frosted gold brown canary. Below: a pair of Norwich Canaries. The clear buff cock and variegated yellow hen are well matched for breeding.

Variegated Buff Norwich Canary. A short but broad outline, a thick neck and a round, wide skull are some of the important attributes of this famous breed.

back. In the 1870's the Norwich breeders introduced the Lancashire Canary, our largest variety which carries a crest, to increase the size of the Norwich. A number of Norwich Canaries then carried a crest which made them resemble the Crest Canary and therefore the standard Norwich is often called the Norwich Plainhead to differentiate.

The Norwich was the first canary ever to be color fed. The story is that in the early 1870's a Norwich breeder had a good bird which had developed a bad chill during the molt and he tried feeding it hot cayenne pepper as a cure. Whether or not this effected a cure is not known, but the bird developed a rich orange color when it grew its new feathers. The breeder kept the secret to himself and after the next molting season produced richly colored birds on the show bench. Predictably, this caused all kinds of trouble and, following protests, the birds were sent to the public analyst, but no traces of artificial coloring or staining could be found. Around 1873 the secret was disclosed and for a period 'fed' and 'non-fed' classes were provided at shows, but it was generally agreed that color feeding had come to stay and the classes were mainly for color fed birds.

Two or three years after the color trouble had been resolved, breeders of the Crested Norwich introduced the Lancashire Coppy into their studs to increase the size of the bird. Soon the Plainhead Norwich breeders introduced the Lancashire Plainhead for the same purpose. This cross was a great mistake that not only introduced coarse feathers into the breed but also altered the bird's shape. Double buffing then became the craze in an attempt to increase the size of the birds, with the inevitable result of feather cysts or 'lumps.' It took many years of ruthless judging down of these birds before the breed was again stabilized, but by then it had fallen greatly in popularity. The correct proportions were re-established by introducing large, well feathered Borders, and after a few generations some first class birds were produced.

Two Lancashire Coppy Canaries (a self green and, in the insert, a yellow). This is a very old English breed which became extinct during World War II but has recently been re-created by 'breeding back' from stock known to contain Lancashire blood which has been used for improvement in earlier years.

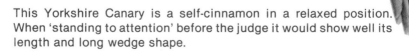

This Yorkshire Canary is a self-cinnamon in a relaxed position. When 'standing to attention' before the judge it would show well its length and long wedge shape.

A broken-capped gold Lizard Canary. In Lizards gold should be paired to silver, and clear cap to broken cap.

The Norwich is not a bird for the beginner to breed. It is very difficult to pair two birds without developing the dreaded 'lumps' or feather cysts. In the 1920's a craze developed once again for size and as Lancashires were not available 'double buffing' was indulged in. This is breeding coarse feathered bird to coarse feathered bird which gives the resulting bird the appearance of being larger, although the apparent increase in size is of course all feathers. The feather produced is so large and soft that sometimes it cannot pass through the feather follicle, turns back inside the skin and forms a cheesy lump. This continues to grow under the skin until the skin can stretch no more and the 'lump' falls out onto the ground. Only by very selective pairing can this serious problem be avoided.

THE CINNAMON CANARY

This fine bird is one of the oldest known varieties, and there is reason to believe that it may have been the first canary mutation. It is now almost identical to the Norwich Canary and indeed at many shows it is included in the Norwich classification. Its coloration is its main peculiarity, with a yellow ground on which brown pigment is superimposed, the usual black color being absent completely. The brown color that results is known as cinnamon, and it produces red eyes in the birds.

Seventy years ago Cinnamons were very popular birds, but by the late 1940's there were very few remaining. Thanks to the efforts of some dedicated fanciers their numbers have increased and the birds are now in no danger of being lost completely to the fancy, but neither are they high in popularity.

THE FIFE CANARY

This variety is in fact a miniature Border Fancy Canary. In the early 1950's many Border fanciers in Scotland were becoming dissatisfied that the 'Wee Gem' was being bred for a larger size and was no longer 'wee.' At the National Show where a miniature class was given there were quite large numbers of small Borders entered and it was evident that many fanciers wanted a smaller bird. In 1957 a meeting was called at Kircaldy in Scotland and it was decided that the bird should on no account exceed 4½ inches in length as opposed to the 5½ inch maximum size of the Border. A new society was formed to specialize in this small bird christened the Fife Fancy in honor of Scotland, where it was and still is heartily supported.

THE LIZARD CANARY

This is the oldest breed that has not changed since it was first developed. Its origins have been lost over the years, but it was mentioned in 1713 by Hervieux. It is the only canary bred for the pattern of its plumage, which resembles the scales on a lizard, hence its name.

The Lizard's head feathers are of supreme importance, and they form what is known as the 'cap.' This is composed of clear feathers covering the head. It should be of even size, nicely oval, and should extend from the beak to the base of the skull. It should not encroach upon the face of the bird as this is a very bad fault known as 'baldface.' Likewise it is a fault if the cap extends down the neck. If the cap is broken by dark feathers it is known as 'broken-cap,' and if the whole cap is obliterated by dark feathers it is known as 'non-cap.'

At one time the Lizard was fast approaching extinction and at the end of World War II there were not thirty known pairs in existence. In 1945 a meeting was held which was attended by all concerned breeders and the Lizard Canary Association was formed to re-establish the breed and bring it once again into popularity. Until this time only birds with clear caps were eligible for show and there were no classes for flighted birds whose plumage tends to carry ex-

Cinnamon colored Border Fancy

The crest mutation. This plain-headed bird, known as crestbred, is the correct partner for a crest.

Spangling on a Lizard Canary.

Opposite:
1. A fancier holds a bird that is perched on his finger. By conditioning his birds to seek their food in a 'different' looking aspect of their environment, this man has taught them to 'think' before they can eat. **2.** Birdroom. **3.** A large number of bird shows are held annually, ranging in size from small local events to large international exhibitions, and the beginner will need to know something of what to expect in the way of competition at the various shows. **4.** This fancier has picked dandelion leaves to feed to his birds with one of their delectables. **5.** Indeed a monstrosity . . . and for the bird a prison! **6.** A very good Corona, with a good center and a good drop. An experienced exhibitor would gently remove the small white feather with a tweezer. **7.** Canaries interest people of all ages.

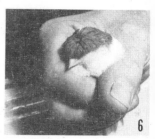

CAGE BIRD BREEDERS
OF AMERICA
The National Cage Bird Society

cess gray after the second molt, both restrictions affecting the popularity of the bird. All this was altered and classes were given for clear-cap, broken-cap, and non-cap, and there were classes for birds of any age. This placed a completely new complexion on the Lizard Fancy, and, as the birds are very free breeders, it was not long before reasonable stocks of birds were available. The Lizard Canary Association went from strength to strength, and now over a hundred birds are entered at some of the leading open shows.

A yellow Lizard is known as a gold and a buff is known as a silver. To further confuse the novice, many special terms are used when talking about Lizards, so the following glossary should prove useful.

Cloudy: Spangling that is not clearly defined.

Eyelash: A thin line of dark feathers over the eye which improves the finish of the eye.

Grizzled: A grayish tint in the plumage.

Lacing: The edging of color on the wing butts and coverts.

Lineage: Straight rows of spangling.

Mooning: Another term for spangling.

Muddy: Another term for cloudy.

Rowing: Markings of breast and flanks. These must be clear and distinct and in lines.

Star Shoulder: The presence of white feathers in the wing butts.

Work: The profusion of markings.

The most important show point of the Lizard is known as 'spangling,' which consists of a series of black spots running down the back and sides. They should be uniform and even, like rows of chains increasing in size and density but remaining dark throughout.

THE ROLLER CANARY

This bird is bred exclusively for its song, and its color,

36

size and shape do not matter in the show ring. Originally known as the German Canary, it was developed in the Hartz Mountains by the four hundred families whose sole business was the breeding and training of these birds. Earlier this century the birds were exported all over the world and were quite rightly considered to be the finest singing canaries obtainable. This bird must have a great deal of training for singing contests, and on no account must it hear any other type of bird song. It is for this reason that the singing contests cannot be held in connection with the usual open shows, for even when adult the birds tend to copy other birds' songs.

The Roller is trained to sing well defined song passages known as 'tours' which are distinct and melodic. The standard method of training originally was to shut the bird in a small cage and let it hear the song of a fully trained bird that was known as a 'schoolmaster.' Today most breeders use phonograph records and tape recordings instead of the schoolmasters. Should a bird develop any faulty tours it must be removed from the birdroom at once or else the other birds may copy the faults.

There are thirteen tours in the British Standard, but few birds can sing them all. The tours are delivered in a continuous rolling manner, hence the bird's name, and most of the tours retain their German titles. Marks are awarded for the degree of perfection with which they are sung. They must be soft and melodious, delivered with the beak almost closed. Judges award marks for the various tours; as can be imagined, the judges must have a good ear themselves.

The Roller Canary's quality of song is partially inherited and partially developed by feeding with a special mixture that is one part canary seed and one part finest rubsen rape with a little mixed condition seed added occasionally. The special rape seed develops the bird's vocal cords, and without this the birds would be useless in song contests. In order to be eligible to compete in any song contest a bird must be wearing a closed metal ring which can be fitted to the leg only when the bird is a nestling. This ring carries the code name of the breeder and the year in which the bird was hatched.

Rollers are very reasonable in price. The hen does not sing but is important to the breeder who is interested in obtaining good stock. When purchasing a male, ensure that it is the correct singing Roller as there are birds called Irish Rollers that bear no resemblance to this sweet songster.

THE CRESTED CANARY

One of the oldest breeds, the Crested Canary has been used to develop a number of other varieties. The bird was originally known as the 'Turncrown,' and its heyday was toward the end of the last century when it was known as the 'King of the Fancy.' It was the great popularity that became the Crested Canary's undoing at a time when a working man's annual wage in England was in the region of forty pounds and it was not unusual for a keen fancier to pay as much as fifty pounds for a single bird! The climax came when a well known breeder paid 265 pounds for three birds; then even the prosperous fancier had to admit that these were indeed the preserve of the rich. Their popularity went steadily down hill from then on.

The two types of Crested Canary are the Crest and the Crest Bred. The Crest Bred carries a plain head as opposed to the Crest, but like all crested birds it is essential to pair crest to plainhead. The Crest is a large bird with a thick, short neck and a broad, deep body similar to a Norwich, but it carries a great deal more feathers than the Norwich. This extra feathering is essential as a good large crest is the main feature of the bird. It should radiate from the center of the head and extend over the beak and over the back of the head, being about level with the eyes, which should not be seen when looking down on the bird. The crest should be shapely, large and dense, with broad feathers of a leafy texture.

The Crested Canary Club is still active and so is The Old Varieties Canary Association. The main objective of the Old Varieties Canary Association is to save the old varieties of canary from becoming extinct. Thanks to the efforts of both of these societies there has been a definite improvement with the Crested and an encouraging increase in numbers.

THE FRILLED CANARY

There are several types of Frilled Canaries: the North Dutch Frill, the South Dutch Frill, the Gibber Italicus Canary, the Milan Frill, the Parisian Frill, the Munich Frill, the Padovan Frill, the Roebekian Frill, the Swiss Frill, the Brazilian Frill, and the Japanese Frill. The Dutch Frill was the original Frill, dating back to the eighteenth century. These were shown in fair numbers, mainly on the Continent, and mutations of this bird figured prominently in the development of the Scotch Fancy and the Lancashire. The largest and most popular Frill is now the Parisian, while the latest Frill developed is the Japanese Frill, a miniature bird that has been extended to the Red Factor. The Frills have made great progress in recent years, and at a recent Old Varieties Canary Association Club Show there were fifty Frills in the four classes provided, the majority being Parisian.

The main feature of all types of Frill Canary is that the feathers curl in a distinctive pattern which is basically the same in every variety. The three major parts of a Frill are the mantle, the jabot, and the fins. The mantle consists of the feathers that are parted down the back and curl symmetrically over each shoulder. The jabot is formed by the chest feathers, which should be undulating and wavy, curling inward and coming from each side of the breast to form a ruffle or craw that meets in the middle like a closed shell. The fins are the long, well-frilled feathers that come from the thighs and rise upward around the wings.

The origin of the frilled mutation is not known, although it is generally accepted that it arose in the old Dutch Fancy. Like the mutation in the Crested Canary, the frilled feathering is dominant in character, and therefore a Frill crossed with any other type of Canary will produce only Frills.

None of the different varieties of Frills are color fed, and although their feathering is much longer than that of any other type of canary they appear to be free from feather cysts.

In a later chapter the standards for the different varieties of canary are given. The Frill Canary has been left out because each type of Frill has its own standard and scale of points for judging. Points desirable in some Frills are penalized when they appear on others. One rather unusual feature about the Parisian Frill is that the bird's toes should be twisted like corkscrews, a feature that would count as a fault with other birds. A good Frill is a most attractive bird, but a bad Frill is such a bunch of unsightly feathers that it can have no attraction at all.

THE BELGIAN CANARY

This breed is not unlike the Scotch Fancy but should not have a circular curve, the back and a narrow piped tail forming a straight line. It has very high, rounded shoulders with long, compact wings braced against the body and a small snake-like head. The neck can be elongated or shortened according to the stance the bird adopts. When viewed in the stock cage the bird appears quite ordinary, but within a minute or two of being run into a show cage it presents a very different picture. If properly trained it will draw itself up and adopt the show position with its neck fully extended and its body erect. A good Belgian is timid, nervous and highly strung, and considerable time must be spent training the bird.

The Belgian Canary is one of the oldest breeds, and it took the Flemish a century to develop it from the Old Dutch Canary. It can claim to be the first bred canary to lose the image of the serin finch completely. Up to that time the different varieties of canary had consisted of color variations, but this bird was entirely different, both in size and shape. It was therefore used extensively in the creation of other breeds, including the Lancashire, the Scotch Fancy, the Frills and the Yorkshire. Although popular at one time in its native Belgium, it has never made a mark for itself outside of its native country and so is rarely seen as a show bird. The bird was never a free breeder and 'feeders' were always provided for its young, which meant keeping a small type of bird as a foster parent.

THE SCOTCH FANCY CANARY

The Scotch Fancy Canary evolved in Scotland from imported Belgian stock in the 1830's. During the 1850's over a thousand of these birds were shown at leading Scottish shows. The hotbed for the bird was the Glasgow area, where it was called the 'Glasgow Don.'

During the latter part of the nineteenth century a great deal of crossbreeding with the Belgian took place with the result that both birds suffered a certain degree of deterioration, and it was apparently quite possible to show a bird either as a Scotch Fancy or as a Belgian. There is little doubt that this was one of the main reasons for the gradual decline of both breeds, and by 1950 the only Scotch Fancies in existence were in Scotland. By 1960 there were no more than twenty pairs surviving.

In the 1970's the Old Varieties Canary Association became active on behalf of the Scotch Fancy. Within a few years their numbers had increased considerably and a definite improvement in quality and type was visible.

The Scotch Fancy is a bird of position and action and should have a jaunty manner on the show bench, not unlike the Border Fancy. It should be a free mover and work the perches with excellent carriage and verve, this requiring considerable training to achieve.

The bird is known as the 'Bird O Circle' and when shown it should form a half circle with its tail swept around below the perch and its head and neck curving down from above. It should have a slender neck with a small head and the shoulders should be high and well filled. It is generally accepted that today's bird is in some respects an improvement on the original bird, which had poor fertility and was more or less useless as a parent, no doubt due to excessive inbreeding. The Scotch Fancy of today has plenty of vigor, good fertility and in most cases is a good parent, but its size is not up to that of the original bird.

THE LANCASHIRE CANARY

The Lancashire is the largest canary, and its original stronghold was in the county after which it is named. In the 1880's at leading Lancashire shows it outnumbered all other varieties of canary. Unfortunately, its popularity did not extend outside Britain except for the hens, which were in great demand by breeders as being very suitable for use in bird hybridization experiments. This local popularity and use in the development of other birds was almost responsible for the extinction of the bird. Its popularity further deteriorated because of the fact that it was never a free breeder or a good feeder and infertility was common.

The Lancashire is a crested canary, but the crest differs from that of other breeds. It is horseshoe shaped with feathers radiating from the center outward over the beak and sides, but the feathers lying down and merging into the back of the neck. This is one feature that present day breeders have not quite perfected as they have used the Crested Canary as one of the parents, but it should be obtainable in time. The body should be long and tapering with a full breast and the legs must be straight and long.

Although it is a clear bird a Grizzled Coppy is permissible. The crested bird is known as the 'Coppy' and the non-crested bird is known as a 'Plainhead.' It is immaterial which sex carries the crest when pairing Coppy to Plainhead.

THE NEW COLOR CANARIES

For several hundred years canary breeders concentrated on type and very little else, but a change has taken place this century—all over the world a great deal of interest is being shown in the New Colors. A German geneticist, Doctor Hans Duncker, published a thesis in 1929 in which he stated that he believed that a red canary could be produced by introducing a red factor into the bird's genetic structure. This was possible because a South American hooded siskin had been successfully mated with a canary and produced a fertile hybrid. The late Mr. A.K. Gill bred the first Red Factor canaries in Britain from birds received from Dr. Duncker, and these proved to be very free breeders. Before long there were quite a few birds in circulation and classes were provided for them at all the open shows. Other colors have been introduced into canaries, so while canaries with hooded siskin blood are termed 'Red Factor,' those with other colorings are termed 'New Color.'

The Canary Colour Breeders' Association was formed in 1947 and a strict ruling was made that no artificial coloring of any kind should be fed to these birds—they must be shown in natural color. It soon became evident that this rule was being broken and that birds that had been color fed were winning at many shows. Many birds purchased off the show bench molted out the following year as very ordinary birds. Something similar happened when a color known as Carophyll Red became available in Europe. This had been developed initially to improve the color in yolks of poultry eggs and had been further perfected to color plumage for certain birds such as flamingos, which tend to

Opposite:
1. Feather characteristics known as Buff (coarse) and Yellow (fine) have nothing to do with color but are used to indicate two forms of feather structure. 2. A Lizard with a broken cap. This photograph (as well of photo #4) shows something of the spangling of the Lizard Canary, although these birds lack a good deal of markings on the shoulder. 3. The Corona is a crested variety of the Gloster. 4. The Lizard Canary is the oldest of all canary breeds. This clear-capped gold shows well the wing markings and the 'spangling' of the back. 5. A Yorkshire hen. 6. English type of Frill Canary cock. Although not a particularly good specimen, this bird shows the dispostion of the basic frills.

---

lose their color in captivity. The Canary Colour Breeder's Association then had no choice but to do an about-face because it defeats the main object of the New Color and Red Factor classes. At bird shows it was common to see a row of birds which looked exactly alike. As 75 points are for color alone, it made the task of the judge very difficult. Fortunately this position is sometimes eased by the fact that too much Carophyll Red gives the plumage a brassy green or even pinkish tinge and any such bird can be marked down.

Lately the New Colors have gone from strength to strength, and at the moment there are about fifty varieties. They are the most popular canaries in Europe and outnumber all other types combined, principally because of the wide varieties of breeding combinations. These birds may be known under a British name or a continental name. As they differ a list has been compiled.

British Name	Continental Name
Melanin Pastel R/O	Pastel R/O Isabel
Melanin Pastel Blue	Pastel Blue
Opal Cinn. R/O Dilute	
Opal Slate Blue˙	Opal Slate
Opal Dilute Green	Opal Agate
Opal Dilute Blue	Opal Silver Agate
Fawn	Silver Brown
Dimorphic Melanin Bronze	Mosaic Pastel Brown

44

The Dutch Frill is a product of Holland. The breast feathers and certain other feathers, instead of lying close to the body as in other birds, actually turn upward and outward, giving the bird a rather frilly appearance. Dutch Frills are not common even in Holland, and they are seldom seen except at canary exhibitions.

46

Green	Green
Dilute Green	Agate
Cinnamon	Brown
Gold Cinnamon Dilute	Gold Isabel
Cinnamon R/O Dilute	R/O Isabel
Dilute Bronze	Bronze Agate
Red Orange Cinnamon	Red Brown
Bronze	Bronze
Rose Pastel	Ivory Rose
Rubino Cinnamon	Rubino Red Brown
Greywing Melanin Pastel Bronze	Greywing Pastel Bronze
Melanin Pastel Dilute Fawn	Pastel Silver Isabel
Dimorphic Bronze	Mosaic Bronze
Melanin Pastel Dilute Blue	Pastel Silver Agate
Rubino Cinnamon Dilute	Rubino Isabel
Rose Pastel Bronze	Ivory Bronze
Phaeo Dilute Cinnamon Albino	Phaeo Albino Isabel
Phaeo Cinnamon Albino	Phaeo Albino Brown
Phaeo Cinnamon Lutino	Phaeo Lutino Brown
Phaeo Dilute Cinnamon Lutino	Phaeo Lutino Isabel
Dimorphic Opal Bronze	Mosaic Opal Bronze
Dimorphic Melanin Pastel Bronze Opal	Mosaic Pastel Opal Bronze
Ivory Pastel	Ivory
Dimorphic Melanin R/O Cinnamon	Mosaic Pastel R/O Isabel
Rose Pastel Bronze Dilute	Ivory Bronze Agate
Opal Rose Pastel Bronze Dilute	Opal Ivory Bronze Agate
Melanin Pastel Cinnamon Dilute Gold	Pastel Gold Isabel
Melanin Pastel Cinnamon Dilute Fawn	Pastel Silver Isabel

Another canary feeding her young. The foods employed by breeders in rearing youngsters consist of soft food, soaked seeds, wild seeds and greenstuff.

Breeding Your Canaries

The ultimate dream of every fancier is a birdroom. This is an attic used by a very successful breeder of show canaries—since he lives in Bristol, these are Borders, of course!!

One of the most interesting aspects of canary keeping as a hobby is the chance to breed your bird and raise a brood of your own. There is no reason why a beginning breeder cannot learn to raise five to 15 birds per season.

Birds are one of the hardest animals to domesticate, and, as tame as they may become, they never feel comfortable when someone is holding their wings, making loud noises or moving about quickly. If you are to be a successful breeder, you must give the birds the maximum amount of privacy and the minimum amount of distraction and disturbance.

The breeding season for canaries begins as soon as spring is in the air. This is the time when the chill is out of the wind, the sun is shining and the risk of losing the baby canaries through cold drafts is down to a minimum. All through the winter the birds have been kept separate and are well fed and healthy, and now they are ready to breed.

BREEDING CAGES

Box cages are the best for breeding. Box cages come as single, double or treble breeders with each cubicle approximately 18" long, 11" deep and 14" high. Double and treble breeders are respectively twice and three times as long as the single unit. The exact dimensions may be adjusted to suit the size of birds to be accommodated and the size of the room. As the name implies, the box cage is simply a box with a wire front.

A double breeder is a form of box cage divided into two cages by means of a wooden or wire mesh slide, and a treble breeder is divided into three sections by two slides. In a double breeder with the slide in position a cock can be placed in one half and a hen in the other so that they can become properly introduced to each other. If placed together without this gradual introduction, fighting may break out. With a treble breeder a cock is placed in the center cage with a hen on each side of him and the same procedure is adopted. By removing one of the slides he is permitted to mate or later help to feed the young in either nest.

Keep the pair separated for a few weeks until they get to know the breeding cage and each other. Then remove the

Opposite:
1. Conditioning of the birds previous to breeding is most important. Start feeding egg food and other soft foods about a month before the breeding season starts. One half-teaspoonful per bird per day is sufficient in the beginning, but you can gradually increase the amount given after the first ten days. 2. The best time to commence breeding is when you see the wild birds beginning to nest in your locality. 3. Just before you commence breeding, keep the male in one side with the solid center partition in place so the birds cannot see each other. The temperature of the breeding room should not be over seventy degrees. 4. Hen near her nest. 5. A pair of Black-hooded Red Siskins. Thanks to these birds we now have the red canaries.

1

2

3

4

5

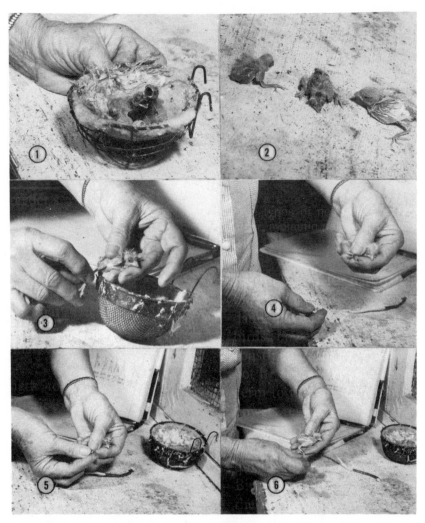

1. Checking babies in nest. 2. The chick on the right is too large to be banded; the one on the left too small; the center chick is just right. 3. Straightening the leg in preparation for slipping on band. 4. Picking up chick to band. 5. Slipping band over leg. 6. The number is recorded and the chick returned to nest.

Three types of nesting receptacle: an earthernware pan with wire holder, a plastic pan and an old-fashioned, though still useful, nest box.

partition and let nature take its course. The diet of the breeders should be supplemented with a little niger seed, dandelion leaves, spinach or lettuce in order to keep the birds' bowels moving regularly. Should the birds become constipated, the female is liable to become egg-bound and not be able to pass her eggs. Add a little olive oil or wheat germ to their biscuit now and then; this too will keep the bowels regular.

It is impossible to say just how long it will be before they prepare their nest and lay their eggs. An important prerequisite to breeding is, of course, the actual mating itself. Birdkeepers utilize the term "riding" when they refer to the male copulating with the female. Once the birds start "riding" you may soon expect to see eggs.

BREEDING TIME

Canaries, like most other birds, lay their eggs daily. A canary will usually lay one egg a day, in the morning. Her entire clutch may run as high as 6 and as low as 2. It is usually much easier for the breeding hen to care for her clutch if the eggs all hatch at the same time, so most

After the nest is complete, you can expect the first egg in eight days or longer.

Opposite:
Gloster Fancy hen with chicks about a week old.

breeders remove the eggs as they are laid and replace them with dummy eggs (these dummy eggs are available at every petshop and department store that handles canaries). The fertile eggs should be carefully removed from the nest with a tablespoon and laid on a piece of cotton. Every day the eggs should be turned over. This should be repeated for the second and third eggs, at which time the fertile eggs are placed back in the nest and the dummy eggs are removed.

Soon after the eggs are laid the hen will spend all her time sitting on the eggs. This is when the male may be removed from the cage or separated from her with the wire partition. During the time the female begins to lay her eggs and for the first week after the last egg is laid, the bath should be removed from the cage. After the 12th day it should be replaced so that the hen can actually sit on her eggs im-

mediately after she bathes. This she does to moisten the egg membranes for her babies, who will soon be struggling inside the eggs to break out. Be sure to keep a close watch over the nest so you will know exactly when the eggs begin to hatch. This is important, for then you must change the hen to a soft diet. This soft food, usually called "nestling food," is available in your pet supply store. To this nestling food should be added the soft part of fresh white bread dipped into boiled milk, the yolk of a hard-boiled egg and a little sweet apple. Be careful the blend does not go sour. This mixture should be offered in the treat cup, while the regular seed is always available in the seed cup. Don't think that one treat cup of soft food is enough for a whole day. Keep your eye on it, and when it needs refilling, make sure that it is refilled.

The idea of separating the male from the female while she is sitting on the nest stems from the fact that sometimes the male may bother the female and distract her from her job. There are many breeders who never remove the male, and they claim that the male actually feeds the female and the young while she is sitting on her nest. This we will leave open for debate and for your own choice. In any case, be sure that you allow the male to get back in with the female after the young are two weeks old, for then the female will surely need help in feeding the baby canaries. Should the female neglect her eggs when you remove the male, be sure to place him with her immediately.

REARING THE YOUNG

The development of the young canary is very interesting. Naturally, when they are first hatched their eyes are closed and they cannot see. It takes about a week for their eyes to open and about two weeks for their plumage to be anything like the adult bird. After three weeks the babies are out of the nest sitting on the perch. When they are a month old they may be taken away from their parents and placed in a separate cage. Usually by the time the young are ready to leave the nest the female is ready with a new batch of eggs, so you have no choice but to remove the babies and get ready for another cycle. It is not too advisable to breed your canaries every time they want to breed. This may result in "breeding out" your birds and they produce weak babies without singing ability. Be selective and only breed the best singers. If you are taking the trouble to breed canaries you might just as well breed the best.

Once in a while a baby bird will die in its infancy. Be sure to remove it immediately as it endangers the lives of the other birds.

Many breeders have closed bands made for their birds with their name and address, code number and year on them. This is a good idea for you, too, for if you sell your birds to a petshop, the only way the dealer will know your birds at a later date is by their bands.

Never be eager to help the chicks to break out of their shells; always leave this to their parents. Human fingers are clumsy at best and at worst could be positively fatal. Leave the parents with the chicks to assist them and interfere yourself only as a last resort.

Before feeding each day it is wise to inspect the cage floor to ensure that none of the young have fallen out of the nest or been accidentally dragged out when the hen was departing. Should you find such a misplaced chick that is in reasonably good condition, breathe warm air onto it while warming it gently in your hands. If a chick appears to be lifeless, do not jump to the conclusion that it is dead, but rather warm it in your hands as mentioned above and keep it near a heater for a quarter of an hour or so until it has fully recovered. Once the chick has been fully revived it should be returned to the nest. A chick that is not in the nest will invariably be ignored by the parents and will soon starve to death. In cases where young are continually being pulled out of the same nest, it may be that the hen's claws are overgrown and are snagging the chicks. The hen may be caught and the claws carefully clipped as mentioned earlier, but it must be remembered that this is not the optimum time to perform this operation as it can quite understandably distress the bird. If the hen's claws are found to be in order, the problem may be caused by the bird flying straight to the perch from the nest. In this case a perch located just above the rim of the nest pan will encourage her to hop slightly when leaving the nest, thus clearing the chicks with her feet.

Some hens will pluck the feathers from the chicks when they are about sixteen days old. Should this occur, transfer the nest to the cock's side of the breeding cage and separate the hen from the cock by the divider. The cock will then feed and rear the young without the help of the hen; this is one of the advantages of pairing one cock to one hen. The hen will probably be getting ready for breeding again and a new nest pan with nesting materials should be supplied to occupy her.

WEANING

After three weeks the young should be removed from their parents and weaned. At this time some of the chicks may still be in the nest, but at the age of three weeks they should be removed. This can be a very trying time for the novice breeder, but it is essential that he hardens his heart and carries out the following. First of all, prepare a single breeding or stock cage and make certain that it is quite clean. Cut a dozen pieces of newspaper to fit the bottom of the cage and fit a very low perch about one and one-half inches above the cage floor. The front of a small wooden tray or feeding board is fitted under the cage door and the rear of the board is supported on a leg to keep it level. In the center of this board place some milk-soaked bread over which has been sprinkled a little maw seed. This turns into black spots, and as a rule the youngsters will peck at these, get a taste for the milk sop sticking to them and from then on all should go well. At times they will refuse to peck at anything and cry for their parents without pause. This is when the breeder must be firm and not return them to their parents or else the second round of young will be spoiled and the youngsters will misbehave for some time. If the birds do refuse to feed, then gently wipe their beaks in the sop to give them a taste of the food. Once a bird starts to feed the others will follow. I like to wean four birds together, but once they are weaned it is best to keep them in pairs to discourage feather plucking. Should any bird be seen to practice this troublesome habit, isolate it immediately and do not let the other birds copy it.

Remove a sheet of newspaper each morning and the birds' droppings will tell you if things are going well. On the second day give some egg food as well as the bread and milk, and on the third day add soaked seed together with a little green food, preferably chickweed if available. On the third day fix two thin wooden perches in the usual positions. On the seventh day and all suitable days thereafter place a bath on the outside of the cage. You can fill the seed hoppers with red rape seed only, and after a few days they should be cracking this freely. Once they are proficient at cracking red rape seed, change to the basic mixture and introduce a pot of grit. The egg food will have been given throughout this period and water should always be available. Although the birds will not drink for several days, it must be there when they want it.

When the young are removed from the nest for weaning, the used nest should be replaced with a fresh one and the hen and cock should be allowed to start their second breeding cycle.

Do not take more than two rounds of young from any one hen in a season and do not allow a round to start after the end of June, as the birds should fall into the annual molt before July is finished.

Approved British
show cage designs;
from left to right:
Gloster Fancy, Nor-
wich and Yorkshire.

Exhibiting
Birds

Exhibiting their canaries is for
many fanciers the highlight of the
years. One can see why . . .

The time will come when the breeder will want to enter his birds in a show to be compared with other birds. There are basically two types of shows, the Open Show and the Club Show, and there are two stages in the Canary Fancy, the Champion and the Novice.

To be eligible to exhibit at a Club Show you must be a paid up member of that particular club. You would exhibit as a Novice and would advance to Champion after winning three classes of eight exhibits or more shown by at least three exhibitors. It is quite likely that you may decide to join two or three local clubs so that you can continue to show as a Novice for the balance of that show season. The following year, however, you must show as a Champion at all clubs unless a particular club has a special rule governing this. No Club Show wins count in any way in respect of the Open Shows, and it is therefore not at all unusual to find Club Champions of long standing still showing as Novices at some of the Open Shows.

The Open Show, as its name implies, is open to anyone who cares to exhibit. Show rules vary little. Usually when you have won three first prizes in classes with eight or more exhibits you become a Champion, but you can continue to show in the Novice classes for the balance of that show season. In the Canary Fancy the rule is that once a Champion always a Champion, so you cannot start again as a Novice exhibiting another variety of canary.

Open Shows are advertised in *American Cage-Bird Magazine* some months in advance. When you have chosen a convenient show at which you wish to exhibit, write to the show secretary requesting a schedule. Together with the show schedule you will receive an entry form which must be completed and returned to the show secretary by the deadline given. The schedule will detail all of the classes for exhibition, and each class will be allotted a number. There will be separate classes for the different varieties of canary and classes will be further divided for flighted and unflighted birds. Great care must be taken to ensure that the correct class is chosen, because a bird entered into the wrong class will be ineligible for judging and the entry fee will be forfeited. When you have established which class your bird should be shown in, this number is entered in the first column of the entry form. Any special labels required for air or hand transport will be specified on the entry form. When the entry form has been duly completed it is returned to the show secretary together with the entry fee.

It is your responsibility to provide the correct show cages and ensure that the birds arrive at the show in time for staging and judging. These can be delivered by hand or sent by air for collection by a show steward, in which case care should be exercised to ensure that the birds have sufficient food and that the steward is advised of their estimated time of arrival. Do not, however, attempt to include a water fountain or you will only end up with a wet cage and a damp bird. If you deliver the birds by hand, the cage together with the listing card is given to the show steward at the door and he will stage and water the bird.

Once the judging has been completed and the show opens to the public, do not hesitate to approach a judge for his opinion of the birds you have exhibited. He will be only too pleased to explain to you why they received the points that they did and may be of invaluable assistance by pointing out to you some fault in your line that you had not noticed. Steps could then be taken to correct these faults.

Gloster Fancy Canary Club's Official Standard of Excellence

CORONA: Neatness; regular, unbroken round shape, eye discernible. 15 pts. With definite 'center.' 5 pts.
CONSORT: Head broad and round at every point, with good rise over center of skull. 15 pts. Eyebrow heavy, showing brow. 5 pts.
Body: Back well filled and wings lying closely thereto; full neck, chest nicely rounded, without prominence. 20 pts.
Tail: Closely folded and well carried. 5 pts.
Plumage: Close, firm, giving a clear-cut appearance; of good quality and good natural color. 15 pts.
Carriage: Alert with quick lively movement. 10 pts.
Legs and Feet: Medium length, without blemish. 5 pts.
Size: For tendency to the diminutive. 15 pts.
Condition: Health, cleanliness. 10 pts.
Total: 100 pts.

The Border Fancy Club's Official Standard of Excellence

Head: Small, round and neat looking; beak fine; eyes central to roundness of head and body. 10 pts.
Body: Back well filled and nicely rounded, running in

almost a straight line from the gentle rise over the shoulders to the point of the tail; chest also nicely rounded, but neither heavy nor prominent, the line gradually tapering to the vent. 15 pts.

Wings: Compact and carried close to the body, just meeting at the tips, at a little lower than the root of the tail. 10 pts.

Legs: Of medium length, showing little thigh, fine and in harmony with the other points, yet corresponding. 5 pts.

Plumage: Close, firm, fine in quality, presenting a smooth, glossy, silken appearance, free from frill or roughness. 10 pts.

Tail: Closely packed and narrow, being nicely rounded and filled in at root. 5 pts.

Position: Semi-erect, standing at an angle of 60 degrees, carriage gay, jaunty, with full poise of the head. 15 pts.

Color: Rich, soft and pure, as level in tint as possible throughout, but extreme depth and hardness such as color feeding gives are debarred. 15 pts.

Health: Condition and cleanliness shall have due weight. 10 pts.

Size: Not to exceed 5 and one-half inches in length. 5 pts.

Total: 100 pts.

Yorkshire Canary Club's
Official Standard of Excellence

Head: Full, round, and cleanly defined. Back skull deep and carried back in line with rise of shoulders. Eye as near center of head as possible. Shoulders proportionately broad. Points rounded and carried well up and gradually merging into the head. Breast full and deep, corresponding to width and rise of shoulders and carried up full to base of beak. 20 pts.

Body: Well rounded and gradually tapering throughout to tail. 10 pts.

Position: Attitude erect with fearless carriage. Legs long without being stilty, and slight lift behind. 25 pts.

Feather: Close, short and tight. Wings proportionately long and evenly carried down the center of the back and firmly set on a compact and closely folded tail. 25 pts.

Size: Length approximately 6 ¾ inches with corresponding symmetrical proportions. 10 pts.

Condition: Health, cleanliness and sound feathers. Color pure and level. 10 pts.

Total: 100 pts.

Norwich Canary Club's
Official Standard of Excellence

Type: Short and cobby. Back broad and well fitted in, showing a slight rise transversely. Chest broad and deep, giving an expansive curved front and sweeping from under therefrom in one full curve to the tail. Ideal length 6 to 6¼ inches. Stance of position at an angle of 45 degrees. 25 pts.

Head: Proportionately bold and assertive in its carriage. A full forehead rising from a short neat beak. To be well rounded over and across the skull. Cheeks full and clean featured, eye to be well placed and unobscured. 10 pts.

Neck: Short and thick, continuing to run from the back skull on to the shoulders and from a full throat into the breast. 10 pts.

Wings: Short and well braced, meeting nicely at the tips to rest lightly, yet closely, on the rump. 10 pts.

Tail: Short, closely packed and well filled in at the root. Rigidly carried, giving an all-of-one appearance with the body. 5 pts.

Legs, Feet: Well set back. Feet perfect. 5 pts.

Condition: In full bloom of perfect health. Bold and bouncing movement. 10 pts.

Quality of Feather: Close and fine in texture presenting the

Yorkshire canary, self green.

The Lancashire Coppy is being revived by keen enthusiasts, notably
G.A. Dodwell, and one stage towards the ultimate goal is seen here.

smooth, silky plumage necessary to give a clean-cut contour. 10 pts.

Color: Rich, bright and level throughout, with sheen or brilliancy. Yellows a deep orange. Buffs rich in ground color and well mealed. 10 pts.

Staging: Clean and correctly staged. 5 pts.

Total: 100 pts.

The Official Standard of Excellence for the Scotch Fancy Canary Established by the Old Varieties Canary Association

Shape: Body long and tapering and curved in the form of a half circle, convex above, concave below, with a clean outline, feather being close, short and tight. 20 pts.

Head and Neck: Small, neat, snaky head. Long, tapering neck. 10 pts.

Shoulders and Back: High, narrow, rounded shoulders, well filled in. Long, narrow, well filled back curving from shoulders to tail. 20 pts.

Tail: Long, narrow, closely folded and well curved under the perch. 5 pts.

Style, Nerve and Travelling: Well raised up, forming a high circle. Bold, free and jaunty carriage, with plenty of life and action. 25 pts.

Size: Approximately six and three-quarters of an inch. 10 pts.

Quality and Condition: Clean, healthy, perfect condition. 10 pts.

Total: 100 pts.

Lizard Society's
Official Standard of Excellence

Spangles (for regularity and distribution): 25 pts.
Feather Quality (for tightness and silkiness): 15 pts.
Ground Color (for depth and evenness): 10 pts.
Breast (for extent and regularity of rowings): 10 pts.
Wings and Tail: 10 pts.
Cap (for neatness and shape): 10 pts.
Covert Feathers (for lacings): 5 pts.
Eyelash (for regularity and clarity): 5 pts.
Beak, Legs, and Feet (for darkness): 5 pts.
Steadiness and Staging: 5 pts.
Total: 100 pts.

The Official Standard of Excellence for
The British Roller Canary Club and
The National Roller Canary Society

Hollow Roll: 10 pts.
Bass: 10 pts.
Water Glucke: 10 pts.
Glucke: 10 pts.
Glucke Roll: 10 pts.
Hollow Bell: 8 pts.
Schockel: 8 pts.
Flutes: 6 pts.
Water Roll: 6 pts.
Deep Bubbling Water Tour: 5 pts.
Bell Roll: 3 pts.
Bell Tour: 2 pts.
General Effect: 10 pts.
Total: 98 pts.

The foods employed in rearing youngsters consist of soft food. A number of brands are marketed under various trade names by pet shops. Some of them are complete rearing foods in themselves and need only preparing according to the maker's directions before feeding to the birds, so that they provide the perfect answer for the busy fancier or for one who is not inclined to dabble in avian dietetics.

Red Factor Canary. A melanin pastel apricot (frosted red) cock.

Canary Color Breeders' Association's Official Standard of Excellence

Color: 55 pts.
Type:
 Body Outline: 10 pts.
 Head: 5 pts.
 Neck: 5 pts.
 Wings: 5 pts.
 Legs and Feet: 2 pts.
 Tail: 3 pts.
Plumage: 5 pts.
Condition: 5 pts.
Staging: 5 pts.
Total: 100 pts.

Cinnamon Canary Club's Offical Standard of Excellence

Color: 35 pts.
Shape and Type: 20 pts
Quality of Feather: 15 pts.
Wing-carriage and Tail: 10 pts.
Size: 10 pts.
Condition, cleanliness, etc.: 10 pts.
Total: 100 pts.

Opposite:
1. Color food is basically finely ground pods of the salad plant *Capsicum annum grossum,* a sweet or tasteless 'pepper.' **2.** In addition to their basic seed mixture, canaries love small amounts of mixed treat-seed twice a week. **3.** Yorkshire canary. **4.** Grizzled Crested Canary. **5.** A nice self green Border Fancy Canary. **6.** The natural molting season usually starts in July and extends until October. Special foods should be provided during this period. **7 & 8.** Approved British show cage design: Norwich.

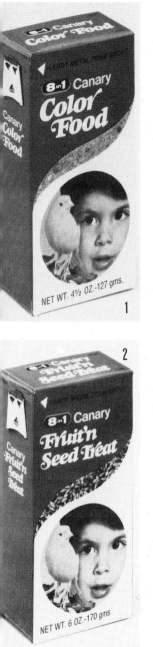

8in1 Canary
Color Food

NET WT. 4½ OZ.-127 gms.

1

8in1 Canary
Fruit'n Seed Treat

NET WT. 6 OZ.-170 gms

2

3

4

5

8in1 Canary
Moulting Food

NET WT. 5 OZ.-141 gms.

6

7

8

Frosted Rose Brown Satinette.

A Roller hen incubating. She is a little apprehensive of the camera and has not yet 'shuffled down' upon her eggs, as has the hen of the photo on page 74.

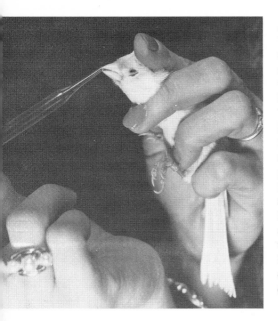

All pet shops carry a full and complete line of proven bird remedies, together with all the different bird seeds, foods etc. There are excellent brand remedies for nearly every canary ailment; they can be procured when necessary and used as directed. Shown here is a method of administering fluid vitamin solutions to birds such as canaries using a dropper or pipette.

Illnesses

A robust canary in good condition. Change in the appearance or behavior of your bird can be a warning of ill health.

Nearly every canary disease can be traced to a cold draft or improper feeding. We can hardly place enough emphasis on the importance of covering your bird at night, of feeding and cleaning the cage regularly and of being certain that the canary is not kept near doors or windows. An ounce of prevention is worth a pound of cure! Remember that . . . it will pay. The following discussions of diseases should be approached with caution. Don't read the list and apply it to your bird, for if you do you'll swear your bird should have been dead a year ago. Know your bird, its actions, habits, song and peculiarities. Only when the bird acts radically different should you think about illness. Then it is much better to take your bird to an expert and allow him to diagnose and treat the bird. This list is merely a first aid chart for use when an expert is not available.

Red orange cinnamon Border Canary.

Opposite:
Scotch Fancy Canary.

WHEEZING, ASTHMA & COLDS

One of the first things a bird will do when he is sick is to sit puffed up like a big ball of feathers and quit singing his song. This is symptomatic of nearly every illness of canaries. In asthma the bird will be wheezing, but this wheezing might not be audible unless you hold your bird's nostrils very close to your ear. If you think your bird is making this wheezing noise when you hold him to your ear, he may be treated by adding a 50 mg. water soluble tablet of terramycin to his drinking water. This same treatment is effective against bronchitis (a dry cough from an advanced cold) and colds (catarrh). For those people who have a large stock of birds, it might be much less expensive if they invested in a quarter pound jar of terramycin for animals. This particular grade of terramycin is helpful for diarrhea too, and it works equally well on dogs, cats, canaries, parrakeets, tropical fish, goldfish and just about every living thing kept in a petshop.

CONSTIPATION

Sometimes a bird's droppings are very hard and black and the bird seems to be experiencing discomfort when passing the droppings. This condition is usually caused by an unbalanced diet, especially the diet where the fresh foods have been omitted for a great length of time. The cure is simple: mix a little castor oil in with hard-boiled egg yolk and feed the bird the paste in the treat cup. Also, give the bird plenty of greens (like spinach, lettuce, dandelion, etc.). A pinch of epsom salts can be added to the drinking water. Be sure that there is enough charcoal in the gravel on the bottom of the cage for the birds, as it aids in the digestion of their foods. If the bird is very bad, give it one small drop of castor oil in its mouth.

CONSUMPTION

This is a general term applied to birds that have been exposed to poor conditions, filthy cages and poor food for a considerable length of time. The bird is feeble, run down, doesn't sing and has no meat on its bones. Usually, when it has reached this stage there is little that can be done for it and the bird dies. The only hope is to give it the best of care, plenty of good, nourishing food, plenty of wheat germ, egg yolk, egg biscuit and a few drops of any human vitamin preparation added to the egg biscuit. Few birds recover when they have reached the advanced stages of consumption, and they usually take cold and die.

CONFINEMENT CRAMPS

Sometimes canaries develop cramps in their legs when they are confined to cages that are too small or when they are forced to stand on wet or dirty perches. If the cramps are in the legs, then merely bathe the legs in a lukewarm bath to which a little table mustard has been added. Give the bird a few drops of olive oil with a dropper. The olive oil treatment is also good for stomach cramps, for when a bird gets cramps in its stomach there is usually nothing else that can be done for it.

DIARRHEA

Diarrhea is a common ailment among cage birds. Generally speaking, it is not a sickness but a symptom of something else. Usually this is stomach upset, but occasionally it can be something more serious. Because of the increased acidity of the droppings, the vent area of the bird will become dirty.

The best treatment is a little terramycin in the water. If this doesn't stop the looseness within a few days, then give the bird one small drop of boiled (but cool) milk every few hours. Usually the diarrhea will stop as soon as the causative agent is remedied. Loose green droppings are a sure sign of diarrhea. If the condition persists take the bird to a veterinarian.

Left: North Hollander (Piebald Slate), strong, large bird. The lightened feathers of the flank make the stout and long feathers distictly recognizable. **Right:** Light Red Isabel, a delicate shade which up to now has been rarely bred.

Left: Blue Lizard. With white ground color the lizard becomes called the "blue." Actually it is "dominant-slate," whereby the cap remains white. Scaling bad. Wing and tail color not good (light edges); likewise not carried close. **Right:** Deep Red, a very attractive and pleasant color for the shower and breeder. The bird shown has an exceedingly unnatural coloration.

Left: Belgian. The pulled-down head and the angular towering shoulder are the main characteristics of the breed. **Right:** Golden Lizard. The individual shown has a wide cap but very irregular scales.

Left: Gloster Fancy Corona. The form should be beautifully round, with all sides smooth. **Right:** Gloster Fancy Consort; the bird shown is outstanding in form and posture.

FEATHER PULLING

This is usually caused by lice. If there are no lice then the bird is lacking in natural oils and its feathers are dry. Give the bird some wheat germ oil added to its egg biscuit and add some wheat cereal to its diet. It may take a few weeks for this feather pulling to stop. Be sure that the bird is not kept in too heated a situation, as heat tends to dry out the feathers. Don't mistake feather pulling for primping, as birds often primp themselves every day for a few minutes. Feather pulling is continuous pulling at the feather.

FEATHER SHEDDING DURING THE WINTER

It is normal for birds to lose their feathers during the molting season from July to November in America and Canada. But sometimes birds go through a false molt, which is dangerous.

False molt is caused by either of two things: incorrect feeding or mishandling the bird. Incorrect feeding must be corrected. Be sure the bird is offered a varied diet with fresh foods fed intermittently with the seeds, song food and egg biscuits. Mishandling is putting the bird in an environment where it is disturbed continually by lights being turned on and off, loud noises or music, glare from street lights, etc., or by being in a very warm room or a room where there is plenty of steam (like a kitchen). This is easily cured by realizing just what you are doing wrong.

Once the bird goes into false molt, it should be moved to another location, kept covered after 6:00 p.m. every night and fed correctly with plenty of molting food, wheat germ oil added to the egg biscuit and a piece of suet hung in the cage.

FRIGHT, FAINTING, FITS
AND OTHER NERVOUS DISORDERS

Fright, fainting, fits and other nervous conditions are usually due to shock of some kind. Overexposure to the sun, a loud noise, a sudden movement and what-have-you are all causes of the bird's fainting and then shaking or dropping dead. If a bird faints, sprinkle a little cold water over it very gently. Then place the bird in a warm spot for a little while in a covered cage.

LICE AND MITES

The lice and mites that sometimes attack canaries are nearly invisible and are hard to find about the cage or on the bird for they hide during the day and only come out at night. The way to detect their presence is to cover the cage at night with a clean white cloth. If there are any mites present, they will be observed as little specks on the white cloth in the early morning. To kill the mites on the cloth either soak it in a strong bleach solution or press it with a very hot iron.

To rid the bird and cage of the mites it is necessary to wait until evening. Then remove the bird from the cage and spray every part of the cage thoroughly with a bird spray. Let the cage dry thoroughly and replace the wood perches and cuttlebone. The cups should be removed and cleaned with hot water. Now take the bird and spray it with bird spray. Nearly all brands do the same job.

LOSS OF SONG

Sometimes a bird will be perfectly healthy and then cease to sing during the summer months. This is not too unusual, for some birds stop singing during the molting season, probably because they feel there is nothing to sing about when half your plumage is gone. The only problem then is to be sure that the bird is well treated so he will sing again. The best way to ensure return to song is to feed the song food every other day during the molt. Also be sure that plenty of wheat germ is offered and that greens and dandelions are available. Sometimes the addition of a little honey to the drinking water helps too. Add some flax seed to the

Left: Deep Golden Yellow. This bird has very good quality of form and color. **Right:** Norwich "Buff." Smooth plumage rounded on all sides must fit harmoniously with the wings and tail in the total picture.

Left: Deep Red Isabel. Unfortunately, the very gross forced red evokes an "unnatural color." **Right:** Paris Frill. The curls stand out more in pale-colored birds.

Left: Red Lizard. Black legs and black beaks required in this difficult piebald breed. **Right:** Slate Opal.

Left: Gloster Fancy Corona. **Right:** Yorkshire, the slender-straight "guardsman" among the canary breeds. Most important: smooth, tight plumage, with wing and tail carried beautifully close.

regular seed occasionally. Be sure that fresh, clean seed and fresh water are offered every single day. This is a very delicate time for the molting canary.

When a bird loses its song when it is not molting, it is a sign something is wrong. Check the droppings, hold the bird to your ear to check for respiratory difficulties, and see whether you can ascertain just what is troubling the poor canary. If it seems perfectly healthy, try a heavier feeding of song food and add a little honey to the drinking water. Sometimes keeping the bird covered with a black cloth for 5 days does the trick.

LOSS OF APPETITE

Sometimes when a bird's diet is changed it will stop eating for a little while. This is not uncommon, for a great many of the large seed companies order their seeds from different parts of the world, and their seeds are not always the same even though they all look alike. Give the canary more song food (or canary treat, as it is sometimes called). Don't worry too much about it for it is rare that a bird starves to death if there is seed available for him to eat.

SCALY LEGS

Young, healthy birds rarely if ever become afflicted with scaly legs. Only the older birds get it, and they should be treated by bathing their feet in warm soapy water for a few minutes and then rubbing their feet gently with some brand of bird ointment (available at your petshop). Usually this treatment, if repeated for a few days, will cause the feet to become normal again.

If the bird's feet are sore and red or the legs are sore, obtain some penicillin ointment from the veterinarian and apply it to the sore area. Keep this up for as long as necessary to cure the condition. Sore feet come from dirty perches or cage bottoms.

SORE EYES

Sometimes a canary will get a cold or an infection in its eye. First bathe the eye gently in a little boric acid solution using a cotton applicator. Then obtain some penicillin ophthalmic ointment from your druggist and apply that to the bird's eye. It should cure the eye within a few days. If a boil appears around the top or bottom of the eye, give it a few days to break by itself; if it doesn't, then maybe it would be wise to gently prick it with a sterile needle. If possible have someone experienced do this job.

BROKEN LEGS AND BROKEN WINGS

If a bird breaks its leg or wing it can usually be fixed. Sometimes if the break in the leg is very severe the set will not take and the leg will dry up and fall off. After a month or so the bird gets along perfectly well on its one leg. To set a broken leg, gently pull the leg apart at the break so you can fit the jagged ends back together again. Then press a soda straw cut to a very short length (about one inch) against the break as a splint. Put some cotton between the straw and the leg. Then a few pieces of Scotch tape or adhesive tape will fasten up the job for the three weeks it will take for the leg to heal.

Perches and swings should be taken out of the cage during this period, for we want the bird to stay at the bottom of the cage where it can easily drag its foot about. The treat cup and seed and water cups should all be placed at the bottom of the cage.

Broken wings are much more difficult to set, so have an expert do the job for you. It is rare that a wing can be set. In all cases, be sure the bird is not disturbed in any way, for the bird realizes how helpless it is and becomes terribly frightened when someone strange approaches the cage.

Border Fancy Canary, a nice self-green. Border breeders are keen on a bird that is as near to grass green as possible.

Border Fancy Canary. A well rounded and nicely proportioned yellow cock.

Upper photo: A Norwich Canary with 'lumps.' **Lower photo:** Feather cysts *(Hypopteronosis cystica)*, fibro-lipoma (benign tumor-top) and osteosarcoma-tumor in the right hand bottom corner.

EGG-BOUND FEMALES

Sometimes a female may be unable to pass her eggs due to a constipated condition. She can be helped by giving her two drops of castor oil in her mouth and gently inserting a few drops into her vent. If this is successful, hold her vent over a steam outlet (like a tea pot), being careful not to scald her. Hold her there long enough for all the skin around her swollen vent to become soft. Please note that these are difficult procedures fraught with great dangers for the bird. If you're not absolutely sure that you can handle things properly without hurting the bird, don't attempt them. Let a veterinarian handle these essentially medical/surgical operations.

The symptoms of egg-binding are easily recognized. The hen may be found in the nest or upon the floor of the cage with feathers all puffed up, eyes half closed and with an utterly 'miserable' look about her. Incorrect mating can also cause egg-binding. The photo above shows a correct mating, a Corona mated to a non-Corona or Crestbred. The photo below shows a very good green Gloster hen.